Mouth and Tongue
Let's Have Some Fun!

of related interest

Challenge Me!™
Speech and Communication Cards
Amanda Elliott
Illustrated by David Kemp
ISBN 978 1 84310 946 4

Attention and Listening in the Early Years
Sharon Garforth
ISBN 978 1 84905 024 1

ISPEEK at Home
Over 1300 Visual Communication Images
Janet Dixon
ISBN 978 1 84310 510 7

Mouth and Tongue Let's Have Some Fun!

Karina Hopper

Illustrated by Lisa MacDonald

Jessica Kingsley Publishers
London and Philadelphia

First published in 2011
by Jessica Kingsley Publishers
116 Pentonville Road
London N1 9JB, UK
and
400 Market Street, Suite 400
Philadelphia, PA 19106, USA

www.jkp.com

Copyright © Karina Hopper 2011
Illustrations copyright © Lisa MacDonald 2011

Library of Congress Cataloging in Publication Data
A CIP catalog record for this book is available from the Library of Congress

British Library Cataloguing in Publication Data
A CIP catalogue record for this book is available from the British Library

ISBN 978 1 84905 161 3

Printed and bound in Great Britain by
MPG Books Group

This book is all about having fun using facial expressions. I chose to write it for personal reasons because two of my children had delayed speech and I found it frustrating that there weren't any books of this kind available. Practising tongue and mouth movements is a great way to strengthen facial muscles and help speech development. I wanted something that was fun and child friendly to capture their concentration and which I could pick up and use on a daily basis.

All children love making silly faces, so I hope this book will be a great addition to any child's book collection. I have also written a second book aimed at helping speech development.

Hi, my name is Sam. I love making silly faces, it's so much fun! I call my tongue "Timmy Tongue". He likes being silly and making funny faces in the mirror with me. Shall we have some fun? Let's go!

Timmy Tongue likes
to tickle my nose.

Timmy Tongue points down to the ground.

Timmy Tongue wiggles
from side to side.

Timmy Tongue jumps up and down.

Timmy Tongue licks a yummy lollipop.

**Timmy Tongue
wobbles like jelly.**

Timmy Tongue plays
peek-a-boo, in out, in out.

Timmy Tongue follows
the shape of my mouth,
round and round.

**Timmy Tongue likes
to polish my teeth.**

**Timmy Tongue likes
pulling silly faces.**

Timmy Tongue needs a rest now. He lets out a big yawn and stretches out as far as he can.

Let's blow some kisses.

Pretend to be a big fish
and blow some bubbles.

Be happy and give
a big smile.

~~~~~~~~~~

Be sad and give an
upside down smile.

~~~~~~~~~~

Be surprised and open your mouth wide like a tunnel.

Be angry and squeeze your mouth together tightly.

~~~~~~~~

Make your mouth disappear!

~~~~~~~~

Now let's give a big smile.
Wasn't that fun?
Well done!

P/6/2223025